Penguin

Color which is the poet's wealth is so expensive
that most take to mere outline sketches
and become Men of Science

HENRY DAVID THOREAU

For my mother
who taught me things I never knew
and my father
who never knew the things he taught me

A season in the life of the Adélie Penguin

Penguin

RECORDED IN WORDS AND PHOTOGRAPHS BY

LLOYD SPENCER DAVIS

HARCOURT BRACE & COMPANY

San Diego   New York   London

Library of Congress Cataloging-in-Publication
Davis, Lloyd Spencer.
Penguin: a season in the life of the Adélie penguin/
recorded in words and photographs by
Lloyd Spencer Davis.—1st ed.
p.   cm.
ISBN 0-15-200070-4
1. Adélie penguin—Reproduction—Juvenile literature.
2. Adélie penguin—Behavior—Juvenile literature.
[1. Adélie penguin. 2. Penguins.
3. Antarctica.]   I. Title.
QL696.S473D39   1994
598.4′41—dc20   93-36407

A B C D E

Printed in Hong Kong

Acknowledgements
A book such as this does not get from conception
to completion without the assistance of many people.
In particular, I was helped by the encouragement and advice
of Barbara Larson, who nurtured this project through its early stages.
My wife, Frances, and children, Daniel and Kelsey, gave me both freedom
when I wanted it and support when I needed it. Jacintha Alexander, my agent,
took up the cause of the book with an enthusiasm that I had no right to expect.
And I am extremely grateful to everyone at Pavilion: Paul Burgess, Stephen
Dobell, Sarah Hinks, Gillian Young and my editior, Julie Davis, for
doing such a fine job while still allowing me the liberty to do it
my way. Louise Howton, Michelle Funk, and staff at
Harcourt Brace helped refine the text. Mostly,
I am thankful to them all for having the
faith to listen to a penguin.

CONTENTS

PREFACE

THE ADÉLIE PENGUIN – *PYGOSCELIS ADELIAE* – SCIENTIFIC BLACK BOX OR CUTESY-PIE CHARACTER IN A TUXEDO? That's all the public sees. Neither is real, neither is relevant. The cartoon image of penguins, portrayed in magazines and natural history documentaries, depicts them as awkward and humanlike. It gives them a lovable persona, but masks their true face. Phantoms of the media.

Science, by contrast, presumes to unmask the truth, but then proceeds to screen that truth from the public (which funds it) behind a barrier of convoluted theory, unnecessary jargon, and a mess of probability values. Reading a scientific paper these days is likely to have all the thrill of reading a telephone directory backward, and in many cases is likely to be less informative. Science has lost its common touch. In an era when specialization is increasingly in vogue, scientists have secured themselves in a self-perpetuating world of narrowly defined journals whose pages can only be penetrated by degrees.

This book is, on one hand, an attempt to make science accessible in a manner that I hope preserves the color of its subject. Throughout its marriage to the testable hypothesis, science has tended to leave the lights off, seldom realizing the beauty it touches. Aesthetics, as well as analysis, should contribute to our understanding and appreciation of the world. Even so, when fleshing out these scientific sketches, I have tried not to lose sight of the facts. These pictures are as accurate as I can make them.

On the other hand, this book has been written in the first person because Antarctica has no other spokespeople. No natives. No citizens. It is up to us scientists who have the privilege of working in Antarctica to act as the mouthpiece for those animals and plants that live there.

It is a delicately balanced web of life that clings to the shores of Antarctica. Break one strand and you weaken the whole structure. I have seen the destruction something as simple as a late ice breakout can bring. But it is not nature's extremes to which Antarctica is most vulnerable. It is the localized depletion of krill, harvested to fatten livestock, and a penguin that needs to forage for a day too long. It is a pesticide dropped on a distant shore finding its way into the eggshells of skuas breeding six thousand miles away. It is an underarm deodorant used somewhere else contributing to a hole in the ozone above Antarctica. It is industrial pollution from another world affecting the melting of the ice cap. It is an oil spill. It is a mining license.

This, then, is not just my view of penguins; in some way, I hope, it represents their view of Antarctica.

ARRIVAL

BLEAK BLACK CLIFFS SHOULDERING SNOW MOLDED TO CLOUD OFFER A POOR WELCOME. In nine summers I have seldom found them any different. Not that I thought about it then, nor care about it now. Sweet or not, this is home. And as my feet trace familiar footsteps, I am drawn to this place of my birth: Cape Bird.

To be a penguin is to be an aquatic bird. Three-quarters of every year we spend at sea among the pack ice. While there we may mingle in large flocks, but come spring each of us returns to our natal rookery to breed. Conditions for breeding are favorable for only a short period, a brief window in time when the shores of Antarctica, if not hospitable, are at least tolerable; a time when parts of the frozen continent shed their winter coat of snow. Each of us must race to complete breeding within that time; a race in which much depends on the timing of our own movements.

But for now, two companions and I walk without haste along the snow-covered beach at the base

of the cliffs. We stop to search the surroundings for scenes imprinted on our memories. We contemplate

cracks that cross our icy pathway for long moments before deciding them safe to jump; the length and

weight of our decision not necessarily governed by the breadth or depth of the crack.

At times on feet, at times on belly, we follow our lengthening shadows along the beach. The gusty

wind into which we walk has shifted the dense cloud, breaking it up and exposing patches of blue sky

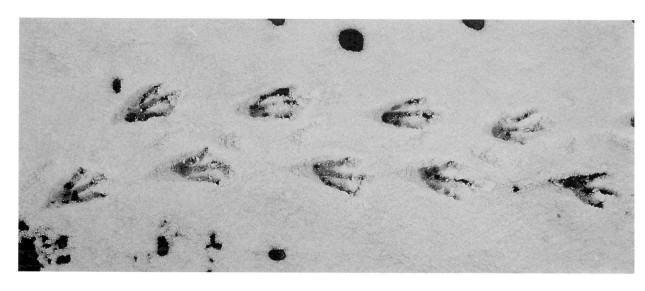

I walk without
haste along the
snow-covered
beach . . .

that darken as the sun drops to our horizon. Poised on distant peaks, the sun becomes an orange ball

whose presence causes remnant clouds to redden.

Lying with my male companions, now swelled in number to six, I remain unaffected by sunset

and snow alike. It is the cycle of the snows that makes it possible for me to breed, and the cycle of the

sun that tells me when to breed. I respond to their changes but do not rejoice in them. I am not known

to these fellows, nor they to me. Nameless neighbors. I have no need for them, yet I stay because they

are of the same feather. It is a penguin paradox that we are all so unsociably gregarious.

The sun has slid down the far side of the faraway mountains for some time before I move away from my brotherless fraternity. Those mountains, witnesses to the promise of my every spring and the deaths that such promises bring. In Antarctica, life and death are never far apart. Without death there would be nothing to sustain life. We live on the edge. It is not an existence that we have adopted by choice, but it is one to which we are adapted.

As I move about, my gait is distinctly awkward. It was not always the way of my kind. Within these flippers that I now hold extended, blood courses through paths to muscle bound to bones, all of which are essentially similar to those that held my ancestors aloft some seventy million summers before. It was then that my ancestors forsook their agility upon the air waves for food beneath the sea's waves. During that period before the evolution of seals and whales, there lay beneath the water a virtually untouched chowder of fish and other seafood delicacies. But large wings and slim bodies did not make for fat bellies, and those with ever more streamlined torsos and stubby wings that could be used to paddle, fished better and survived best. Thus we penguins were born.

I stop dead. I am standing atop a ridge. My feet sit wedged between slippers of stone and shale. Feet and stones are embedded in a layer of snow. There is no visible advantage to my position, yet I know this to be a prime site, and over the years have paid a high price to get it, and a higher price still to keep it. My nest is my home – my only possession – and from this one I have repelled many who would steal it. It lies among forty-three others that, when the snow melts, will be revealed as a single oval-shaped colony.

I move my head from side to side. There are four other adults at their stations within this colony. Each as belligerent as me. Each with the indignant air of possessing something of importance. Yet each seemingly possessing nothing. They are probably all males, since usually most of us males arrive at the

rookery every summer ahead of the bulk of the females. However, even to me this is not immediately obvious. Females are no fairer than males in my species. We all look alike; it is only with recourse to voice or behavior that I am able to sustain my dynasty.

I move twenty paces or so, bend down, and pick up a small rock. My action is so un-hesitating and deliberate that you might sup-pose that I went to get a rock that was one in a million. And I did. It lay amid scores just like it. Stone and head held high, I return triumph-antly and cast the stone into the empty depres-sion that is my nest, as if stating that I am with-out sin. I have stolen nonetheless. For the stone has come from the as yet unoccupied nest of a neighbor. As the number of adults in the colony increases, so will the crime rate. We Adélie penguins spend much of our time, while in our colony, either protecting the stones that form our nest or stealing them from others.

. . . it being the prerogative only of males to sing the *ecstatic* call . . .

. . . the ice ship belonging to my mate and her fellow black-and-white sailors.

Those poor unfortunates on the periphery of the colony fare worst. For their stones are stolen by those birds just inside them, which in turn lose theirs to others inside them. Overall, there is a movement of stones to the center of the colony, where nests are more lavish than those of the peripheral dwellers, who must get most of their stones from outside the colony, often by stealing from the peripheral nests of other colonies. It was not for nothing that I fought so hard for my central position.

I puff out my chest, throw back my head, and bill pointing skyward, spread my flippers. Then with a rhythmic pumping of my chest and a waving of my flippers, I shatter the stillness of Cape Bird: "Err Err Err," building to a crescendo, "Errrrrrr." It is an advertisement. A song of self. And it is contagious. Three of my neighbors do likewise and sing their songs, thereby indicating that they are of the sperm producing gender: it being the prerogative only of males to sing the *ecstatic* call during the courtship period.

Out at sea, or rather, out at ice, my voice goes unheard, at least by my mate. She is too far away. She marches. Marches with two dozen others across what, to her eyes, appears to be an infinite piece of pack ice. She marches anyway. There is an end to everything, and at the end of her journey will be Cape Bird, me, and my song. She navigates with the aid of the sun's position and an internal clock, which together tell her in what direction on the Cape her would-be serenader lies.

The wind is getting stronger. Pack ice creaks and groans, cracks and moans. Flurries of snow, driven at speed, buffet my partner and her group.

Back at the colony I am taking the brunt of the storm, and I am taking it lying down: eyes closed, head pointing into the brutal winds that lash at feathers and face alike. Unable to do much else, I merely lie here and wait for the storm to abate. Which it does.

The huge head rises out of the water like some sea monster— which it is.

Fingers of morning sunlight grip the crevassed slopes of the ice cap. The shadow in which I have been standing retreats. For a fraction of a flipper beat I am dazed. During the entire summer breeding season, it is never dark at Cape Bird. However, the sun does venture behind mountains during its daily travels: initially those far off ones, hugging the horizon, leaving rose-washed clouds in its wake. Later in the season, as the sun sits higher and the circle described by its passage through our sky becomes smaller, only the mountain at the back of our colony will be able to block its rays for awhile on a cloudless day. This cycle of the sun, this relative change in light intensity – from shadow world to sunlight – marks the days of the summer somewhere in my brain. Not that I make a point of assessing the light, it is all the same to me, be it shadow or sunshine. To an Adélie penguin, all is absolute: our world is black-and-white, so to speak.

From the sun's present position, as it rounds the mountain, the consequences of the storm would be obvious. A large lead, or channel, has opened in the pack ice close to shore, exposing an expanse of dark blue water. The pack ice itself has been broken into pieces that jigsaw together in mute testimony that it had once been whole. Moderate northeasterly breezes are moving this giant puzzle offshore.

I tuck my head into my shoulders, blink, and look about. Eleven others are in my colony now. Beyond them, on either side, I can make out the burgeoning numbers of penguins at other colonies; some smaller, some many times larger than this.

My partner raises her head. It had been resting on her shoulder while she slept, bill tucked under her left flipper. Leaning forward, she stretches, body and neck extended, flippers held hindward, bill open in a yawn. Settling back, she surveys her surroundings.

She is moved by them. Not because of the beauty the setting commands, but because the slight wind has shifted around to a more northerly quarter and is gently steering the pack ice on which she sits toward the nearby shore. In the bite on the southern side of a small ice promontory that juts into the Ross Sea, the water is protected from the breeze, effecting a rolling surface as smooth as the new ice on a freshly frozen pond. It is into this serene sea that my partner's ice boat now drifts. Complete calm. Silence is accentuated by the muffled slapping of pack ice as it rises and falls in the ever-so-slight swell. Occasionally those on shore pollute the air with their *ecstatic* calls.

With an angry dying flourish of color and energy, the sun, precariously close to being consumed once more by the mountains across the sound, paints golden yellow the bows of the ice ship belonging to my mate and her fellow black-and-white sailors.

PSSSHH! The calm explodes. Destroyed by the hiss of expelled air, ruptured by the crunching of small pieces of ice that carpet the sea's surface. The huge head rises out of the water like some sea monster – which it is. It inspects my mate and her group. Those at the edge of the floe panic, scrambling toward the security of its center. The leopard seal dives, then reappears, nostrils flaring, on the other side of their icy refuge. No penguin morsel is to be had, and the hungry seal leaves to check on the dozen or so other groups of Adélies marooned on similar pieces of pack ice.

Tension slowly subsides aboard my female's floating fortress, and she is once again able to turn her attention to the surroundings. To the south, the sky seems stained with blood, silhouetting the jagged outline of a stranded iceberg. Without emotion she realizes that she is almost home.

It is not just her home. Although she cannot know the question, nor its significance, there resides here the answer to the meaning of life itself: here among the moving ice, the setting sun, the hunted penguin, and the hunting seal.

COURTSHIP

HUMANS CAME TO THIS LAND IN SEARCH OF SUCH AN ANSWER.
Most, it seems, found only more questions. Antarctica is the keeper of
many secrets, and many have paid for the privilege of learning, with the
pain of empty bellies and frostbitten toes.

Fortunately, those men that came initially to tread the surface of
Antarctica were not intent on destroying her. It was a period of dog sleds
and discovery, of hunger and heroes, of triumph and tragedy. I did not
see them come, but with my own eyes I saw the remains of those who
would not leave. At the end of one summer's luckless breeding, I journeyed south along the coast of our island before making landfall in a bay
in which I determined to molt. There I found shelter beside a weathered
wooden hut. Sunlight fell upon its windows, possibly warming its interi-
or as it had its occupants some eighty summers before, I didn't know. But

outside, in a chill wind that penetrated through to the very shafts of my newly formed feathers, I saw only signs of death: a cross upon a hill, an abandoned sledge and a dog in agonized repose, still tethered – luckily, judging by its teeth. These were men that gave their all, and took with them only knowledge. They sacrificed ships, fingers, and lives in exchange for that knowledge. Scott, Wilson, Bowers, Evans: names carved in wood of men who never returned to that hut and their still-waiting beds. And it seemed Oates would not be back, even given some time.

Today's lesser heroes struggle to survive in skidoos and helicopters. Instead of answers, they seek oil and gold and whale meat. Despite the sun never setting throughout their summer sorties, most human visitors to Antarctica that I have seen remain peculiarly in the dark. They scar her body with their airfields, kill her animals, urinate on her snow, and violate her depths with their drilling rigs. In the name of science. In the guise of the military. In the pursuit of politics.

For the moment, at least, none of this touches my female as she stands with a companion on the push ice, their breasts glinting in the sunlight – the dress whites of those newly returned from the sea – silently at attention before the sweeping panorama of Ross Island's northernmost penguin rookery. The push ice forms an interface between land and sea: it is solid water that separates that which is not solid from that which is not water. It is a legacy of the Antarctic winter. During that longest of long nights the surface of the sea freezes, and under pressure from storms it is broken, battered, and pushed on top of itself at the sea's margins. With spring's warmth the pack ice departs, leaving behind this wall of jumbled ice blocks. Throughout summer, the action of sun and sea will steadily erode the ice, eventually exposing an expanse of shingle beach beneath. Right now, however, the sun is doing little more than warming my penguin and her partner.

... names carved in wood of men who would never return ...

It was during the twilight time, as the sun journeyed behind the mountain that overlooks our breeding area, that the wind shifted once more, driving my mate and her ice floe along the shoreline of the rookery. At last her icy vessel came to rest, its further progress impeded by fast ice. There followed a long, anxious period before she took the plunge, swam a few short penguin lengths of open water, and leapt upon the push ice; the leopard seal, the Ross Sea, and a long dark winter behind her.

Before her now, the snow-draped land rises in steady undulations. Along each ridge, black dots attest to the unevenness of the ground, as penguin colonies form on areas that, if not now, will soon be free of snow. Behind the colonies, sharp-sided moraines provide a backdrop for the rookery.

The moraines are the remains of an age of ice, the discarded garbage of glaciation. These particular moraines were formed by our nearby mountain's ice cap: a vast sheet of crippled water that even now hobbles from mountain peak to sea. Sliding behind the rookery, it is a huge tongue that the land pokes out at the sea, ending in spectacularly sheer ice cliffs some seventy penguins high. In the shelter of these cliffs, the sea ice has not been broken up, and it is this ice which had brought a halt to my female's wandering floe.

My penguin gazes to her left at the foreboding black clouds, which contrast against the whiteness of the ice cliffs in true penguin sense of decor. Beyond the furthermost tip of the ice tongue, the bump of an island can barely be discerned among the cloud. Whatever weather such portentous clouds may hold will be kept away from the rookery by the southerly wind. But this is of little concern to her as she jumps down from the push ice and joins a line of Adélies walking single file along the shore, away from the cloud-shrouded ice cliffs, on her way toward me, and getting closer all the time.

It is not a long way. Before a rocky outcrop, she steps out of line. A few stop with her, but after a moment's hesitation scurry to catch the rest of their file, which heads resolutely southward in the direction of two other rookeries nestled between the cliffs of Cape Bird. Adélies are born followers, never leaders.

Right: Behind the colonies, sharp-sided moraines provide a backdrop for the rookery.

Left: Adélies are born followers, never leaders.

Left: . . . she stands with a companion on the push ice, their breasts glinting in the sunlight . . . .

To her left, up the steep incline of the beach and onto the sides of the moraines themselves, lie colonies scattered in a pattern all too familiar to her. It is the neural imprints of her own feet that she now follows, as she walks between colonies taking a path long since etched in her memory. Negotiating *ecstaticing* males and the outstretched beaks of her fellows, my female finally halts before me, an upright black-and-white image of herself and those around her.

At first I give no outward sign of recognition. She steps forward even closer, her head slightly bowed. I stand stoically facing her, the erect mantle of feathers at the back of my neck my only acknowledgment of her presence. Swiftly, then, I bend down toward her and, simultaneously calling to each other, we raise our heads, weaving them from side to side. Bill to bill, throat to throat, chest to chest, we face the sky and the new summer with the *mutual* song of a pair reunited. It is our song, our embrace, our way of reinforcing our pair bond.

Mutual calls are like fingerprints. We can distinguish the calls of our mate from those of our neighbors, and those of our neighbors from those of strangers. In this way, despite our outward uniformity, we can treat each other differently. It is not that all penguins are not hatched equal. I know only that I must compete to survive, and reproduce to be successful.

We penguins are what you might call serially, as opposed to seriously, monogamous. We may take only one partner at a time, but we take it whenever we can get it. Males set up the nest site, then court any female that comes within a glacier length of the colony. We are not very discriminating: fat ones, thin ones, young and old. For what do a few million sperm matter to us – there are plenty more where they came from. But for the females it is a different story: they produce only two eggs and have only one chance. Get it wrong and the season's breeding is blown. So while we males will mate with anyone, the choosiness of our females ensures that we get to mate with virtually no one. The image of our court-ship – that of male combatants fighting among ourselves for the spoils of war – is far from the truth. We are more like starved chicks begging for a morsel.

And our females are discerning providers. If they are going to risk investing their parental aspi-rations with a male, then better to lessen the risk. If they have been successful previously, females pre-fer to retain that male, which they recognize by his *mutual* call. To facilitate reuniting, females first return to their old nest site. However, the exact timing of breeding is crucial for success in the short Antarctic summer. It does not pay to wait for old mates not yet back on their nest site, no matter how good they were, and a female arriving at the colony will pair almost immediately. When taking a new mate, females choose us partly by the way we sound. Big fat penguins make the best partners, and big fat penguins have low, flat sounding *ecstatic* calls.

Should a female arrive to find her old mate paired already, she may drive the interloper out with a blaze of beats from her flippers. Should a female take a new mate and subsequently have her old one return, she may abandon the new one for the old. In these ways, it is not uncommon for female Adélies to couple with two or even three partners per season. And for some of us with the testes, that means there is also the possibility of getting to mate with two or three females. Some males, though, mainly those wretched individuals holding ineptly to nests on the colony periphery, do not get to breed at all. There are more adult males than females, and what can you do if you've never been successful, if you've never been anything but thin, if you sing only in falsetto.

I bred for the first time in my fifth summer. That liaison was short-lived, our single egg being lost within days of laying. At the beginning of the next summer, I engaged another consort and joined with

Opposite: Battles are fought, and blood is spilled.

Right: . . . we face the sky and the new summer with the *mutual* song of a pair reunited.

her for three successive breeding seasons. The next summer she failed to show, perhaps fallen victim to the wily leopard seal, the grueling Antarctic winter, or maybe she was just late to arrive that summer. Whatever, it was then that my current mate, a virgin of three summers, had been attracted by my *ecstatic* calls. This would now be our fourth summer together.

The black clouds, which were harassing the island to the north, have dissipated – perhaps pouring their scorn and snow on worlds beyond our horizon. In our world the sun raises the air temperature to an unseasonable degree just below freezing. The wind is all but absent, save for the occasional pathetic puff that dares to ruffle the smooth surface of the sea. The sea itself is visible only in the small leads between floes of pack ice, which have closed in on the beach in dense formation. On one of the floes a leopard seal lies sunbathing, no doubt on a full stomach of Adélie penguin. Taking advantage of the seal's lassitude, groups of porpoising penguins swim quickly and safely across the open leads. By now there are over thirty birds in our colony. In a few days there will be nearly a hundred, while in the rookery as a whole, nearly sixty thousand.

This is the courtship period. The rookery reverberates with the raucous calls of *ecstaticing* males, *mutualing* couples, and the staccato sound of flippers beating bodies. We get only one opportunity to breed each summer. To be successful, we must mount or be mounted within our first dozen days on shore. The beginning of the breeding season sees the rookery in a frenzy, with old mates fighting for each other, new mates fighting for another, and unattached mates fighting with each other. Competition.

It is called the *arms act*—but this is love not war.

I lie in my bowl of stones, feathers sleeked so as to appear slender and nonthreatening. With my left foot, the one nearest and visible to my partner, I rake the stones, scraping them outward. Mine is a symbolic gesture, for the nest is already complete, the hollow already formed. I am not constructing, I am consorting. Penguin foreplay is feet first. Head deeply bowed so that my bill virtually touches my feet, I stand, and then move to one side. This is the moment of truth: the time when Adélie ardor can be cooled or fanned. If she takes the nest, I take her; if not, I don't.

She does not hesitate. Head bowed to the right degree, as if responding to the exaggerated bowing of a lesser mortal, she moves onto the nest of stones. Bedrock. I edge around to her side as she lies down and proceeds to arrange some of the pebbles about her. With bill still near my belly, I jump atop her back. My mate arches her head backward as I begin to vibrate my bill against her bill and throat.

Flippers forward and down, I wave them frenetically, erratically above her back. It is called the *arms act* – but this is love not war. The vibrations stimulate my mate as I pad my way along her back, causing her to hold her tail aloft, exposing the pulsating cloaca. In an instant – a fleeting instant – I bring my own tail down over her rear. Cloacal contact. The products of some seventy million summers of evolution pass between us in less than a heartbeat. I hop down and stand beside her, my gaze fixed on a distant horizon, as she continues to lie prostrate in the nest. Both of us give the appearance of nothing having happened; our proximity to each other the only clue to our recent cloacal coupling. We can be caught in cloacula regularly thereafter for the next several days. All around there are females to court and fights to be fought. The whole colony is either fighting or reproducing.

Colonial life remains frantic throughout some fifteen cycles of the sun. Males *ecstatic* at frequent intervals. Pairs continue to copulate at only slightly less frequent intervals. Stones are found, and stones are lost. Battles are fought, and blood is spilled. The most serious disputes are always those over either sites or spouses. This is the courtship period. This is life.

INCUBATION

SNOW FALLS SOFTLY AND INCESSANTLY. I stand up and shake the layer of delicate crystals from my back. Each snow crystal is like a tiny anemic starfish. They do not compact but remain poised on my feathers. My slightest movement and they drop to earth like a shower of chick down. No matter how many times I stand, shift, shake, and shuffle, the falling snow quickly replaces that shaken loose. My appearance is constant, even if the snow is not.

The total absence of wind is greatly preferable to the howling southerlies of earlier days, though it means the total absence of sun, too. The clouds carrying the snow cover Cape Bird completely, merging with the pack ice, leaving the horizon without definition. It is a softly focused world. A world without highlights. The sea in a lead close inshore reflects the flat gray of its celestial covering. As snowflakes find the surfaces of the rookery's black rocks, they too reflect as gray. Overnight our penguin world has changed from black-and-white to shades of gray.

For the most part, I lie on my eggs, keeping them warm. Despite my coat of snow, I am warm, too. Without wind, even temperatures below freezing are mild by penguin standards. My female has been gone now for eleven days and, as I wait for her, my impatience grows as my fat reserves dwindle. Every now and then I stand up and *ecstatic*, either at my own instigation or in response to my fellows. Only now I often culminate my *ecstatic* calls with a loud *mutual* call, cried out while looking at the eggs. My eggs. Her eggs. Where is she?

The eggs were laid, three days apart, in what can only be described as difficult circum-stances, even by my standards, hardened after twelve summers and winters spent in Antarctica. If experience has taught me one thing, it is that the weather is never pre-dictable. Certainly summer is milder, but it can often be more erratic, and in its way as potentially lethal as the severest cold that winter has to offer. In fact, it is wind and not cold that is our deadliest foe. Calm days can be positively balmy. Windy days can kill.

Bent well forward, one behind the other, seeking what shelter they could from the body in front . . .

The dark male skua also long calls from his position on the nest.

Early in the season, when eggs are being laid, is perhaps the most unsettled time of all. Storms can appear as if by magic. Now you see them, now you don't. Typically they come from the south, charged with speed and bite, racing over the mountains that line our horizon, en route to their victims.

The sun had circled twice through the sky after our first egg had been laid, when the breeze swung dramatically to the south. It stiffened, gathering momentum quickly. Our random orientations changed quickly too, as we responded to the windchill by presenting as small a profile as possible. We cannot calculate a single statistic, yet we respond to changes in our environment with absolute precision. Temperature, wind speed, wind direction, sunlight, and snow: we react to all, moving our bodies and adopting positions that help regulate our internal temperatures. All of us lay facing into the wind. No need to calculate that this was the position that produced the least wind resistance and lost the least heat: it was simply a matter of head on it was cold, side on it was horribly cold!

Ordinarily such conditions would have been uncomfortable, but not unbearable. Then, however, the wind continued to build, blasting our faces with volcanic sands. Waves bashed at ice floes. Spume slashed across the beach like horizontal rain.

From the height of my colony, I watched a line of penguins, bent well forward, one behind the other, seeking what shelter they could from the body in front, as they tried to march southward in the direction of the next rookery. Others on the icy foreshore lost their footing and fell, as they had not done since they were day-old chicks learning to stand.

For nearly half a day the wind raged. Unpaired birds and several attending partners left the colony, either to find shelter in the lee of cliffs or to go to sea. That was not too unusual. What happened next was. The wind changed from rage to scream. It literally blew penguins from nests and eggs from colonies. Then, as quickly as it had arrived and wrought its destruction, the wind died, leaving us quiet, still.

The snow was black with embedded sand. Penguin eggs lay scattered on the northern side of colonies. Those not completely frozen were being eaten by skuas, quick to capitalize on their windfall. Over half the eggs in our colony had been lost. The sturdy construction of our nest and the slight protection afforded by our central position had kept our lone egg safe within its stone walls. Fortunately the storm had come at a time when pairs had, if they had begun laying at all, only a single egg like us. We lay two eggs, usually three days apart, although young or inexperienced birds will sometimes lay but one. For those that had lost their first egg, there would at least be a chance to lay another.

Our second egg arrived the day after the storm. Soon afterward, my mate left me, eggs tucked into my brood patch. I was left to incubate, while she went to sea to feed, exhausted from the days of courtship and the energy demanded to produce our eggs.

Dawn. My colony has been in its regular phase of shadow when the first of the morning's rays touch the corner of the colony. A short time later and I am bathing in the sunlight – my first such bath in several unseen cycles of the sun. Earlier, the cloud that had enveloped us for the last few days vanished. While its high-altitude cousin still obscures the view to the south and west, for the moment the sun is free to make its presence felt. And feel it I do. Its warmth is absorbed through my black back.

I have been sleeping, bill tucked under flipper. I stand, stretch and yawn, flap my flippers, then shake my head. I begin to preen. First nibbling the feathers on my breast, next rubbing my head against an outstretched flipper, then prodding at the base of my tail, and so on – leaving no feather unturned. I settle down again in my nest, being careful to keep the eggs on my feet and against the skin of my brood patch.

Something inside my body is telling me it is time to feed. Yet I stay. It is a curious balance between surviving and reproducing, between having protein or having progeny. All but one nest in the colony is occupied by males incubating eggs, awaiting the return of their partners. A single nonbreeder still stands his ground; the rest of the unsuccessful males have gone to sea, opting for protein having failed with progeny. I stand and *ecstatic*. As my body fat burns, I end this song with a fiery *mutual* call. The warm air expelled from my lungs frosts, forming a tiny cloud that flies over my head toward the moraines, its course determined by the very light and unusual westerly breeze. Almost always at Cape Bird, the wind blows either from the south or the north.

During the shadowed time that preceded the sun, a male in a nest adjacent to mine deserted his eggs. Starving, skinny, it being a long time since he had last fed, he was unable to wait any longer. Throughout his last day on the nest he had incubated only halfheartedly, standing over the eggs, only half protecting them. At last he gave the eggs a final peck, then stalked off toward the sea, defeated.

Now, the first female returns to the colony. She is from the pair that was earliest to complete laying, and she has been away for nineteen days. There is much *mutualing* between her and her mate, and then she takes over the nest. For a while, in the morning sun, her male remains. Soon he will search for stones, then he too will go to search for krill.

Temperatures are cool once again, the sky gray, once again. Yesterday's sunshine has been but a relaxation of the retina; a passing dream. I can no longer remember being warm.

Of my six nearest neighbors, two have already given up the wait for their spouses. Punctuality is so very important for the survival of our eggs and chicks. The females at sea must get back before their males get too hungry and desert. Timing. All that remains of my three departed neighbors are empty depressions in the ground: their eggs going soon after them. Gone to the skuas.

Patiently, quietly, head always moving, eyes always searching, the skua sits just beyond the pecking range of a large male on the northwest edge of our colony. The light tawny color of her breast melts into the guano-stained and penguin-trampled earth on which she

In half that
instant it is
gone.

sits. Her dark brown colored mate incubates their two eggs in a hollow on a small rise overlooking my

colony, and not more than a wing beat from it.

When the skua first approached the colony there had been several grunts from penguins signaling

alarm. The big male nearest her, and the penguin in the nest next to his, stared sideways at the skua, their

crests erected. Penguin posturing. Penguin propaganda. They were threatening, but she was the threat.

The big male shuffled to his feet, disturbed by her presence. But it was his eggs, not his legs, that she desired.

Another skua swoops low overhead. The female automatically, involuntarily, thrusts back her

large wings and shouts her long call. It is the voice of ownership. She is declaring, "This land, this colony,

and even this egg are mine." Simultaneously, all heads in the colony start and look around at their feath-

ered foe. In response to his mate's call, the dark male skua also long-calls from his position on the nest.

"*Ahh Ahh Ahh Ahhhhhhh Ah Ah Ah Ah.*"

Disturbance is the skua's chief ally, and now the tawny-breasted bird uses the unsettling effect the

long calls have on the colony to her own ends. She takes two steps closer to the large male penguin. Alarmed,

he stands again, half stooped over his eggs, twisting his head from side to side. This *alternate state* is part

aggression, part anxiety. The skua makes a quick, decisive, but intentionally ineffectual probe with her

beak. She did not mean to get the egg, merely to upset the male. Again a quick stab. The male twists on his

nest. He gapes. He thrusts his head forward trying to peck the skua. In doing so, his balance goes forward

with his beak. The fast eyes of the skua see the beak well in advance. She feints to her left, then darts to her

right. Off balance, the male lunges. He falls forward. Bill collides with stone not skua. For an instant, one

egg is partially exposed at his side. In half that instant it is gone. Penguin egg in bill, the tawny skua flies to

her mate – for a meal that never tasted so sweet.

If skuas are the scoundrels of our penguin colonies, they are the sweethearts of the skies. They are to flight what whales are to big. Acrobats. Aeronauts. Entertainers. On the wing they make other birds look lifeless.

Grappling, twisting, two bodies collide. Scratching, pecking, and flapping, they plummet together toward the rocky ground. The first breaks away, missing the stony surface by a feather, and climbs high into the dark blue evening sky. The second is only marginally behind. The first skua twists again, rolls to its left, and pulling its wings close to its body, dives deeply, cutting through the air at startling speed. The second sees the first turn, times its roll but an instant later, and pulling its wings in a fraction tighter, it rockets toward its target. As they swoop low over my colony, the air rushing through their primaries

As chicks, if they have an older sibling, they will almost certainly be killed by it.

sounds like the military aircraft I see, ever more frequently now, ferrying latter-day Scotts to our shores. And military aircraft is exactly what they are. The skuas arc upward, and the second catches the first, slamming the weight of its body and the momentum of its flight into the unprotected side of its foe. There is a small crack. The clavicles snap. And the first skua falls to the ground, wings outstretched.

A patch of snow softens the fall, but not the attack. Instantly the second skua is on the pursued one's back, pecking with vicious stabs of its barbed bill. It drives its bill through feathers and muscle, through splinters of bone, into the air sacs below. Air escapes with a hiss, followed by blood, which drenches the exposed red flesh. The vanquished bird flaps uselessly, trying desperately to escape the ruthless chopping of the bill searing its back with pain and knifing bloodily at its head and cheeks. Snow wets the feathers on the side of its face, like the tears of salt that dampen the cheeks of a beached Weddell seal. The skua is dying and it knows it. Its last breaths are great gasps of air, sucked through nostrils only to be lost through the torn hole in its back.

Skuas don't just kill each other – they even cannibalize their own. There are too many of them. Too many to get suitable breeding positions at least. Consequently, they are fiercely territorial, with others always waiting in the wings, as it were. The non-territorial skuas form clubs, where they congregate like boisterous adolescents learning their trade: how to kill. Killing is something

Speed enough to hurl themselves right out of the sea, four penguin lengths up . . .

they live with, like the feathers on their backs. As eggs they are likely to be stolen and eaten by other parents. As chicks, if they have an older sibling, they will almost certainly be killed by it. While relatively few adults are killed, the margins for error are small in aerial combat, and each summer I walk past more than one broken skua carcass at the base of the Cape Bird cliffs.

Most skuas get their sustenance from the sea. Those whose territories encompass penguin colonies, however, will either supplement their fish diet, or usurp it altogether, with penguin eggs or penguin chicks. In our own way, while we don't indulge in infanticide or siblicide, we are equally lethal for our progeny. In many respects, we are our own worst enemies. As many eggs may be abandoned by us as stolen by skuas; and nearly as many chicks may die of starvation as those torn asunder by a skua's bill. It comes down to timing, time and time again.

Pack ice closes in on the shores of Cape Bird once more. Where ice does not abut, the intervening

She sparkles in the mauve light.

sea is encased beneath an opaque crust, its surface having frozen overnight. Ominous blue clouds shroud the mountains in mystery and misery to the south. What foul weather they hold, what frightful temperatures they herald, I am not to know. At Cape Bird the air is without form, lifeless. Sea ice, pack ice, and sporadic patches of perfectly still water all reflect the cold-bearing cloud as warm mauve.

My mate emerges from under an ice floe, into the placid waters near the shore. She grunts to a companion and together they dive, swimming beneath the frozen and fractured surface with great speed; speed enough to hurl themselves right out of the sea, four penguin lengths up, onto the push ice.

She sparkles in the mauve light. A tire of blubber sits like a collar around her throat. During her eighteen days at sea she has increased her weight by a quarter. There are two types of penguins: gluttons and dead ones. To get through the long fasts associated with incubation, and later to feed our chicks, we must eat for today and tomorrow.

My shadow has time to move to the other side of my body before she arrives at the colony. As she climbs the slope to our colony, high on the side of the moraine, the wind freshens from the north, holding those blue clouds at bay. She stops at each colony on the way up, to get her bearings, but once at our colony she does not hesitate. She walks directly and quickly up to me. She expresses no surprise at the ease with which she can walk between nests due to the gaps left by those that have been abandoned. She cannot fail to express, however, her enthusiasm for being home: she breaks into our *mutual* song when still several paces from the nest. I respond in kind, alternately waving my head about hers and then singing down at our eggs. There are several movements to our singing, each punctuated by a pause and then a *quiet mutual*, a sort of whispered groan, for the coda.

After a little while, head bowed, she nudges me gently as I lie on the eggs. I shuffle to my feet, then shuffle aside, looking all the while at our eggs as I do so. She immediately takes her place in the nest, carefully prodding the eggs with her bill, pushing them against her blood-warmed brood patch. My long first incubation spell has ended. The second has begun.

I stand by the nest and shake myself. I preen. During the fast I have used up most of my fat. I am famished. I am also parent and partner, and not about to neglect my duties. For a while I stand by the nest, on occasions bending down to give my mate a *quiet mutual* as she lies stretched across our eggs. I collect pebbles, taking them from a nest that was deserted yesterday. I drop the stones at her side, and return to fetch another. And another. Until our already well-formed nest resembles nothing less than a large hill or a small mountain. Then, one time, I do not return. I leave. Gone without a good-bye, I just walk down the hill. On my way I stop at a snowbank to eat huge gulps of snow interspersed with appreciative grunts. Over long periods of incubation our bodies become dehydrated in the dry Antarctic atmosphere.

FORAGING

As I make my way down the slope, I notice that for the first time in twenty days or so, a large expanse of open blue water is visible. Even now it does not extend too far. It is bounded on three sides by the white of pack ice, stretching in unbroken brightness to the horizon. Push ice forms the foreshore boundary. The lead is nevertheless the largest seen in the densely packed waters surrounding Cape Bird since the big storm early in the season.

I can see small bands of penguins, mainly males, departing for the feeding grounds: their black bodies streak the flat blue surface of the sea with shadows and ripples. Every now and then, groups of females come porpoising through the lead with agitated speed. Whether their haste is precipitated by pursuing seals or is merely a pander to punctuality, I know not. They are late nonetheless.

The consistent, gentle northerly winds, such as stir my feathers now, though more benign in touch than those screaming winds from the south, threaten the rookery with a calamity far greater than that exacted by any storm. They have driven pack ice, from here to the horizon and probably beyond, hard against the shores of our island. And while females after laying must go to sea to fatten, they must also get back in time to relieve their thinning mates. But crawling across ice on belly and feet is far less effective than swimming, free and fast. Also, the almost perpetual covering of ice has delayed the bloom of the phytoplankton, those minute vegetables of the ocean that depend upon summer's sunlight and that ultimately support nearly all life in Antarctica. No phytoplankton means no krill. And no krill means traveling even farther north to find food.

The females feed until full. Until they have reached a threshold, a lard line, a sort of minimum

... a female Weddell seal raises a sleepy head ...

level of fat. So in summers when the sea is open to the rookery and the krill are abundant, their first foraging trips may last just fourteen days or less; in summers like the present one, they may be away for twenty-one days; and, in rare instances, even longer. Together with the time ashore during courtship, we males are forced to fast for up to thirty-three days. And that is about as long as any Adélie can fast.

On reaching the beach, I join several of my comrades grouped on the push ice. Their dirty breasts and lean bodies testify to their sex: they are males like me, leaving their guano-

and dirt-stained nests after their long enforced diet. Nearby a female Weddell seal raises a sleepy head in response to the series of grunts that accompany my arrival in their midst. Weddells often beach their blotched bodies on our shore for a little rest and relaxation. We do not mind their presence, except when one of them lumbers through our nests. They are fish eaters. Perhaps not our pals; mostly not our enemies.

Right now it is another seal that concerns us. Not its presence, just the mere possibility of its presence. In this group of a hundred penguins, only one or two of us will fail to survive the attention of leopard seals this summer, whereas a quarter of us will not survive the coming winter. And yet we display more fear of entering the water – our one avenue to food – than we do of that deathly darkness. A group of penguins porpoise by. We call excitedly and jostle. A few dive in. The rest of us hang back, not quite sure of ourselves, not quite certain of our safety. I have heard it said that we push one of our fellows in, to test the waters so to speak. Nonsense! Our hesitancy, our jostling, our calling, the fact that we may leave a few at a time before being followed by hundreds en masse – it may look like sacrifice, but in reality it is only a sign of our indecision.

Another group swims by. More calling. More jostling. We bunch up. Then, like a black-and-white waterfall, we hurl ourselves off the overhanging edge of the push ice.

The water is cold and clear. Empty of virtually all but sounds. The eerie wails and clicks of seal sonar reverberate about me. The sculptured sides of ice floes, translucent to the sunlight, press down into the water.

There is no time to appreciate this beauty. Suddenly I am in the air, sunlight flashing from my back, catching a breath of air, before another few quick strokes of my flippers underwater. Porpoising is the fastest way we travel. Once beyond the margin of the rookery, where the danger of leopard seals

Then, like a
black-and-white
waterfall, we
hurl ourselves
off the over-
hanging edge of
the push ice.

is greatest, I pause with my school of fellow voyagers to bathe and then dive hungrily for the krill that float in clumps one hundred penguin lengths below the surface. Krill are the staple food of Antarctica, feeding fish, seal, penguin, and whale. At times I have seen water so thick with their red bodies that you might imagine it to be the blood, not the food, of a thousand blue whales. Though, these days, there is little chance of that; most of the whales bled to death long ago.

Porpoising is the
fastest way we
travel.

Even though I am wracked with hunger – weak with hunger – there will be little enough time to feed. Nearly twenty days have passed since our eggs were laid; our chicks will hatch in another fourteen. Without food they will die. It is imperative that I return with full belly before they hatch, because my partner, fasting on the nest during her incubation spell, will have nothing to regurgitate but her voice.

Whereas the risk for a female of being late from her first foraging trip is that her mate will desert, the risk for us males is that our chicks will hatch and starve. Females lessen the risk of the former by choosing big mates with sufficient fat reserves to survive an extended fast. They do this by either remating with us if we endured the fast the previous season – they are unlikely to give deserters a second chance – or by listening to our *ecstatic* calls. The bigger we are, the deeper our voices; the fatter we are, the more attenuated our highest frequencies. To female Adélies, a low and flat voice is desirable: they don't touch tenors.

Therein lies the catch though, for us tuneless basses. The longer we fast, the more of our fat reserves we burn up, but the less time we have available to restore them. We must get back before our chicks hatch, and if necessary, that means we must cut short our feeding. To help us, we have an internal timer that allows us to adjust our period spent away from the nest in relation to the time remaining until our chicks hatch.

Our clock is set at the end of courtship. When we stop copulating our ovaries and testes wither without use, and the levels of our sex hormones plummet. It is a signal to our body that incubation has begun. But there needs to be an alarm, something to tell us when the eggs are done. So after this first lot of hormones has disappeared, taking our sex drives with them, another lot rises in anticipation of our chicks hatching to stimulate parental behavior. If we are at sea and get this call to fatherhood, we stop feeding and return to the nest.

I jump aboard an ice floe to rest. Soon I will leave to travel north, past the small island visible from our rookery, where experience tells me the krill are in greater abundance. By the time our chicks hatch, with the succession of summer, krill will be dense in the waters around our rookery, allowing us to feed the chicks on a daily basis. I look across at an adjacent ice floe. A couple of crabeater seals lie stretched out, resting too. The parallel scars, where the teeth of killer whales have raked their bodies, are visible even from here. While killer is an appropriate name for whales that gorge themselves on pale-bodied seals, crabeater is a complete misnomer. Like us, these seals feed almost exclusively on krill.

Stiff southerly winds swat my mate as she lies on the nest. She catches a glimpse, a flash, of white. She looks

out: out over the ice cliffs, to the small island beyond – the direction of my travels – and then, closer in, to

the push ice dividing the shore from the wild sea. Another flash. Gone. There again, against the blue sea,

its form given substance for an instant, the brilliant

white of a snow petrel. In her four previous summers

at Cape Bird, my partner has seen not many more than

twenty snow petrels; before this day is out, she will

see not many less than two thousand. Something

about this unseasonable southerly has brought the

darting, delicate creatures from their nesting grounds

on the distant island, along our beach. All are head-

ed south, flying into the unyielding winds.

. . . the brilliant white of a snow petrel.

The snow petrels are only a quarter of the size

of the skuas. Their flight is erratic: turning and twist-

ing, ducking and diving, alternately flapping then glid-

ing. Their thin wings reflect the sunlight as they cut

the air like a leopard seal's canines. But what gives

them their ephemeral character is not their size, not their shape, not their flight: it's their color. Or rather,

their lack of color. Whiter than white. As they dart along the push ice, one moment my mate can see them

above the waves; the next, they have magically disappeared, lost in their background of push ice. Later, as

the wind settles from a different quarter, the petrels fly up the moraines, passing directly over her head.

Far left:
Crabeater is a complete misnomer. Like us, these seals feed almost exclusively on krill.

Left: An emperor penguin moves with stately steps that speak not of caution but of grace.

Only their little black beaks, their little black feet, and their little black eyes that look quickly at my partner,

destroy the impression of perfect whiteness flashing over her head. White lightning. Antarctic angels.

Slowly, surely, the number of eggs in the colony dwindles: stolen by stealthy skuas, deserted by hungry

parents, or hatched into hungry chicks. Thirteen cycles of the sun have now passed since my mate relieved

me on the nest. Pain gnaws at the inside of her empty belly, telling her to leave, as the eggs adhering to

the outside of her body provide the stimulus to stay.

Just this afternoon she has watched another female stand up and walk away from her nest. But while

there is some danger that males will not get back from foraging before their partners' fat reserves are deplet-

ed, the real concern, as the end of incubation approaches, is that the chicks will hatch and starve to death.

Already my mate can hear the sounds of chicks begging for their first meals. During the time of shadow that

passes for night, chicks at three nests in the colony hatched. Matted masses of gray down with black crowns,

they weigh only a fraction as much as my mate, but in little more than forty days will need to weigh even

more than her if they are to be given a chance of surviving their first winter. This is a rapid rate of growth, but

possible, thanks to an abundance of krill and the continuous daylight that permits us to forage all the time.

But all the krill and all the time in the world won't help our chicks if I don't get back to the nest by

the time they hatch. Our chicks will hatch with the remnant of the yolk sac, their source of nourishment

while in the egg, still attached to their circulatory system. It provides a sort of insurance. With the yolk, they

can survive unfed for up to six days. Insurance can provide only so much protection, however, and many

Adélie chicks starve to death around their sixth day. They starve not because of lack of food in the sea, but

because a parent has failed to bring it to them; and very often that failed parent is their father.

I have been alternately fishing for krill and resting on pack ice in a zone well to the north and west of the small island. Though I'm still not fully rejuvenated from the punishment that more than thirty days without food exacted from my body, I am getting messages from within. I turn for home.

Now, fourteen days since leaving, I am back. The air is calm, the threat of a storm written across cheerless clouds to the south.

Negotiating the ice block jumble that is the push ice, I round a block to find royalty. At least the closest we get to it. An emperor penguin moves with stately steps that speak not of caution but of grace. Slow, gentle, unworried. Emperors breed during the very heart of Antarctica's winter, walking egg or chick about on padded feet to insulate it from the fierce cold, and huddling together to protect themselves from the same. They, too, must carefully coordinate their foraging trips, and as it takes longer to trek to their feeding areas across the frozen sea ice, they must fast longer: for more than a quarter of a year if they are males. I'd walk a little slowly too after all that. This one, having finished breeding, is probably looking for a sheltered place to molt.

Over the lip of the slope at the colony's edge, I march toward my partner. She *mutuals* to me when I am still three outstretched flippers away. I *mutual* back. Throat near throat, we cry to each other.

I bow my head and shuffle even closer. She *mutuals* at the eggs, steps off them, and lets me take her place. My foraging trip has finished; soon my partner will begin another. It is a peculiar fate that we penguins have been dealt, destined by our design to swim and feed at sea, but doomed by our past to breed on land: for as birds we must lay shelled eggs that must be kept warm, and such eggs cannot survive at sea. So we live this double life, separating sustenance from sex. Be we emperors, Adélies, or any other kind, we must find the right balance between feeding and fasting if we are ever to hear the voices of our offspring.

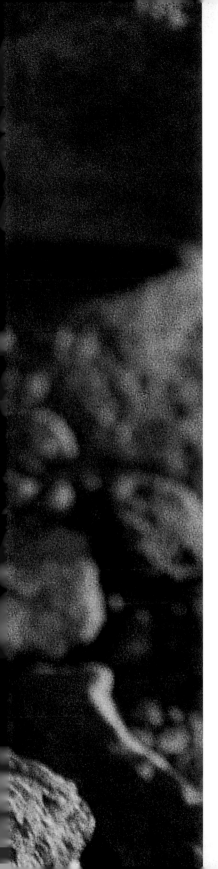

CHICKS

SOUND COMES FROM MY FEET. Little cheeps. I stand and look at my eggs. Both have small round holes, punched by the white egg tooth on the tip of my emergent chicks' bills. Although the eggs were laid three days apart, the first was incubated only partially until laying was complete, and our progeny will see the light of the same first day.

I feel the slight expansion in one of the objects nestled between by webbed feet and body, without hearing the cracking of shell. Tucking my bill down, I see my first chick, its down not yet dry. It responds to my movements by lifting its head and begging in a plaintive voice.

A large, flat ice floe crashes into the push ice, splashing me with its sound. Apart from the scattered ice debris that results from such friction, the sea is naked halfway to the horizon – a layer of pack ice preserving the modesty of its nether regions. The sea is deep of color and reflective of mood. Only schools of porpoising penguins disturb its calm.

My mate will be among the agitators. Like me, she has a hormonal timer to keep track of incubation. In summers when the seas are open and we complete the first two foraging trips in double quick time, say around twenty-six cycles of the sun, she will take five, or even seven further cycles on this third foraging trip. But not this year. High levels of hormone pumping through her blood have already switched her from long foraging trips to short ones. It is important, once our chicks hatch, not only that there is food for them then, but that there is food every day thereafter. So from now on, she and I will swap places on the nest virtually on a daily basis: one going to sea, while the other is left on guard duty.

During the first days of their tenuous existence, our chicks must be guarded against the ravages of cold and the ravenous skuas. Their circulatory system and downy covering are insufficient to insulate them, even in these, the most mild of Antarctica's days. It will be some fifteen days before they can regulate their own body temperatures.

My second chick has hatched and joined its voice to its sibling's. I muffle their cries by lying on them. I pant. For me, at least, it is too hot.

Cape Bird is breathless with beauty. Pack ice drifts imperceptibly southward in the calm. Each fragment reflects perfectly on the mirrored surface, so at first glance there appears to be double the ice and half the open water.

The sun does not set but its light softens with the passing of the day, turning from white to gold. On shore, penguins feed chicks or listen to their begging pleas, while their mates porpoise through the water in search of more food. Across the sound, huge mountains lie fogged in cloud.

It is into this placid panorama that Cape Bird's longest and briefest visitor appears. At first it is just a small black convex dome that breaks the surface skin of the sea. Sun reflects from it as a flash. White gold. The dome grows larger, and from it erupts an inverted cone of silvery mist. Then, like some giant wheel, the great leviathan body arches through space – its dorsal fin pathetically small and out of place on the black expanse of back. The gently rolling body eases itself back into its seawater sanctuary before its tail flukes can break the surface. In the space of four or five heartbeats it has come and gone. Now, only rings of concentric ripples, as they spread out symmetrically toward the chaos of pack ice, indicate by their epicenter where our gargantuan guest has been. They too fade, surrendering to the dampening effect of the ice. The majesty of its movement, the magic of that moment, is all that remains of the sei whale. Like most of Antarctica's whales, it is a creature threatened with extinction – because, to another creature, gold is worth a good deal more than grace.

I mince-walk into the center of the colony. By sleeking my feathers, stretching my body, and walking on tip-toe, I appear thin and harmless. That way I am able to negotiate, without getting too many pecks, the ring of aggressive unemployed birds that surround my nest – those unsuccessful breeders who failed either to get eggs in the first place or look after them in the second, and who return to the rookery at this time of year to practice the rituals of parenthood, such as nest-building and courtship. Arriving unscathed at my nest, I shrug off this effeminate facade and assume a much more macho stance. Me: provider, protector, parent.

I *mutual* loudly with my partner, who has been standing guard over our chicks. A neighboring pair, without chicks, is disturbed by our *mutualing*, and while the male *ecstatics*, his mate *mutuals* quietly.

. . . our chicks must be guarded against the ravages of cold and the ravenous skuas.

My chicks, sensitive to their meal having just arrived, pester me, begging for food by vibrating their bills

on the underside of my throat. For the moment, I am more the harried parent than the willing provider.

Crest raised, face feathers sleeked, I move in tight circles to avoid the entreaties of my chicks. Wheeling,

in this the beginnings of the fledgling dance known as the feeding chase, I bump into the couple next

door. They peck and gape at me. I immediately don my protector cap, dealing one a peck and the other

a decent few blows of my flipper. Turning to my still whining chicks, I submit to their urgings, and by

reflex my stomach convulses. Dinner is served.

Within a short time of my arrival, my mate has left. Our chicks are twenty-one days old, and we

are among the few parents still guarding our chicks continuously. When chicks reach this age, such are

their appetites that typically both parents must be away fetching food. Our chicks can now regulate their

own body temperatures, they can recognize their own nest site, and most

important, they can recognize the voices of their own parents. For

we only feed our own.

The early morning air is damp with the expecta-

tion of snow. Blue-black clouds sit above the

pack ice like giant bruises. My chicks

huddle together. It is now that my

need to abandon them battles

with my urge to guard them.

I leave the nest a couple

. . . begging for food by vibrating their bills on the underside of my throat.

of times, walk to the colony edge, and then quickly run back, *mutualing* loudly to the chicks. After a third such farewell, I walk down the hill, entrusting my chicks to the care of colony and crèche.

Chicks left unguarded congregate in crèches. They seek each other's contact when temperatures drop, but mainly, they hang out together for the protection from persistent harassment by skuas that comes with being in a group. This summer, with many nests lost to storms, skuas, or deserting parents, more unsuccessful adults than usual have returned to the colony at this time. The arrival of these birds tends to coincide with the period when the chicks are first left unguarded. They do not actively protect the chicks, but by their mere presence, typically around the edges of the colony, the attentions of skuas can be thwarted.

In my absence, my chicks continue to huddle on the nest for some time. The chickless couple from next door starts prodding and pecking them with soft nips of their bills. The chicks disperse. They run into more pecks and, finally, into another couple of chicks: a crèche is born.

A blustery day. Wind reaches from the north. A sun, pale and wan, hangs somewhere above the wind where its warmth cannot be felt. It is a rare sight. During the past ten days we have seldom glimpsed the sun, swathed as it has been in solid gray cloud.

The one bright note has been the development of our two chicks. They now weigh only a little less than us. Our experience, together with our central nest site, has provided them with the unlikely gift of survival. A central nest is only an advantage until crèching, however, as we are about to learn.

Returning from a successful feeding trip that might have taken a day, perhaps a year – who can tell in these dayless days, these nightless nights – my mate runs to our nest and gives a loud *mutual* cry. Our two chicks peel off from their crèche and run, helter-skelter, to their mother.

A crèche is born.

The skuas, still
able to get the
odd chick.

Immediately they begin to pester her for food, shaking, vibrating their bills beneath hers. She walks, they follow. She runs, they follow. Always begging, always hassling, always vibrating. She turns and flees to the edge of the colony, face sleeked, the picture of frazzled parenthood.

It happens almost without her knowing. Too quickly for her to act, too quickly for her to prevent it. A flash of feathers. Dark brown. The skua grabs the biggest chick by its bill and pulls it over the bank at the colony's edge. My mate gives chase, a few paces, no more: instinctively keeping near her colony and her other chick. An unemployed bird also runs at the skuas, for now there are two: one still pulling the bill, another pulling a floppy flipper. This only encourages the skuas to pull the chick farther from the sanctuary of the colony, the safety of the crèche – sealing its fate.

They peck, they pull, they plunge. Violent thrusts of their bills stab the back of the chick's neck, tearing first the down, then skin, then muscle. The chick's legs kick in spasms as a skua's bill batters through its spinal cord. No more pain. The other skua pecks at the chick's bowels, carelessly disemboweling it. Death. A slow brutal death. Skuas' bills are adapted for fishing, not finishing penguins off. Even so, with penguin chicks about, they often find that the fishing is best within our colonies.

My partner continues to feed our remaining chick. It is as if an event too shattering for her to comprehend has occurred. The chick may rest in peace, but there is no loving memory. Gone. Forgotten. No questions. Because there can be no answers.

It has happened like this before, and it will happen like this again. Three summers ago we raised two chicks to nearly crèche stage, only to lose them, one after the other, to skuas. It must seem strange in a land so outwardly barren, that skuas and not starvation should be the major killer of our chicks. Chicks do starve, but only when parents fail to return in time to feed them, not because there are too few krill. The demise of the whales has seen to that. Those gentle beasts with their gigantic appetites are our competitors for the krill, and in their absence we have more krill than we know what to do with. And our bountiful food supply seems destined to increase as the slaughter of the whales continues. Not now the butchered giants; now the smaller minke whales.

These last couple of summers I have seen fewer of the minkes' brown bodies arching slowly through the water, their angular dorsal fins, perhaps as high as me, curved backward. I have seen fewer of their knotted foreheads breaking the surface and blowing upside-down cones of backlit spray into the evening air. Every now and then a great jaw with pale throat would push upward, and there used to be the sound of their blowing in the distance, like the muffled crash of ice breaking off the cliffs at summer's end. They are losing this battle, having already lost the war. Their silence is a poor substitute.

Not now the butchered giants; now the smaller minke whales.

Even with the death of the whales, even with the abundance of krill now on our doorstep, there will come a time this season when starvation will threaten. By then the push ice will have melted or been moved away by the surf. Titanic bergs with chiseled sides will advance from behind the ice cliffs, recent émigrés from a much larger sheet of ice, the ice shelf. Weddell seals will come to take up station along the beach like dead slugs of monstrous proportions, their only hint of life an occasional movement of a flipper to scratch a cheek or nose. They will caterpillar up the beach, barely extricating themselves from the surf before falling asleep. And then, caught by another wave, they

will move, prodded and pushed by the sea, until they are finally asleep on the dry black gravel. It will be a time when the last of the season's sun will reflect from snow clouds, providing spectacular lighting to the north – a backdrop for the bergs and a warning to us that the season is nearly past, our race nearly over.

The colonies will have substantially broken down. Scattered nest stones and earth stained red with our krill-laden waste will be all that is left to mark the previously sacrosanct boundaries of the colonies. Adults and chicks alike will be able to walk through the colonies with impunity.

Far left:
. . . a warning to us that the season is nearly past, our race nearly over.

Below: . . . winter's curtain of snow-storms . . . threatening season's close . . .

Chicks will move to crèches in other colonies or join those forming in the land between. The chicks will be clumped around one or two remaining adults, if any remain, and where not, they will stand even closer together as skuas sit nearby. The skuas, still able to get the odd chick.

The number of penguins in the rookery will drop precipitously as parents stay at sea to fatten in preparation for their molt; as the other adults leave to begin molting; and as chicks, left alone to fend for themselves, congregate on the beach in anticipation of their first swim.

The chicks will be virtually free of down, a topknot or a patch of gray across their shoulders perhaps the last to go. They will stand for long periods on pieces of remaining ice, looking at the sea, approaching it, only to stand and look again. Adults will arrive ashore infrequently now, singly or in twos and threes. Optimistic chicks beg from any wet adult that will pause long enough to hear their pleadings. At best they are likely to receive a peck for their troubles. Eventually, drawn by hunger, pushed by instinct, a group of chicks will jump in, swimming with heads up, as if afraid to put them under. They will call excitedly to each other and slowly head out to sea, a sea from whence they will not return for at least two summers.

They will leave behind them molting adults, standing on the beach with loose feathers hanging precariously. Though most of us prefer to molt in the shelter of valleys or the lee of cliffs found farther inland or around the coast, many simply stand near the water's edge if the winds are not too severe. Our feathers are our survival shield. They insulate us from Antarctica's cold, isolate us from her freezing waters. To be effective they must be kept in good condition. Preening can do only so much, and each year we must replace the old feathers with new ones. Therein lies the rub: the process of molting is itself debilitating.

Feathers cost. They cost us time to produce, and mostly, they cost us energy. And all the while we must do without effective insulation and do without food, unable as we are to go to sea. So we look for shelter and stand still to conserve heat, to conserve energy. It is important that we get through the twenty days of molt while the weather is still amenable to our undress. It is important that we are fat enough at the start of the molt to fuel our fast, and form our feathers. If our bodies run out of fat to fire their needs, they will start to burn protein, and our only source of protein is our muscles. Muscles, the things that make us move. And what use are fine feathers if you cannot move? What use is a good-looking corpse? Hence, as winter's curtain of snowstorms hangs across the horizon threatening season's close, we will need to choose a moment to stop feeding our chicks and fatten ourselves, ready for our molt and the winter migration ahead. Through the darkness of winter we will journey far to the north, away from the Antarctic continent. It is a perilous journey, and if we are to survive it, there must come a time soon when we put ourselves before our progeny.

In the end, the rookery will be deserted. Storm clouds will gather overhead, while reddish sunsets appear in open sky to the south. Bleeding carcasses of starved chicks, ripped apart by the skuas, will dot the ground as snow begins to fall. That is the fate of those too slow to fledge. Right now, therefore, we race to feed our chicks, because we are running out of time.

Bleak. Bleak like yesterday. Bleak like tomorrow. Clouds still hang about, their silver linings, if any, invisible to us. For the most part, we have our heads underwater anyway. Fishing for krill. We are not fishing together; my mate has been at sea for longer than me. Having dived repeatedly in the deep waters of the sound with some forty companions, she now heads back to the rookery, her belly brimming with red krill. Mother's milk. Ahead she can see the white cliffs of the ice cap that delineates the northern border of our rookery. Home is but a short swim away, heaven but a few strokes.

Chicks . . .
congregate on
the beach in
anticipation of
their first swim.

. . . most of us
prefer to molt in
the shelter of
valleys or the
lee of cliffs . . .

The process of
molting is itself
debilitating.

At first all she hears are the staccato echoes. The penguins stop swimming and paddle on the surface. For a flipper beat, maybe two. One of the leading birds utters an alarm call. With great gulps of air, perhaps their last, they dive and scatter, swimming for their lives.

Instantly it is among them. As if it has always been with them. Like as far back as she can remember. Dark as a shadow, it pursues her as surely. My mate twists and turns. Her group has fanned out.

Half through their own confusion, half to confuse their would-be hunter. She hears rather than feels the cracking of the bones in her chest. A clavicle parts company with her sternum, the *crack* having more of a *pop* sound underwater.

Then she feels it. A scorching pain that rips down her left side. Her left flipper dangles uselessly. But she is free. Beating frantically, fiercely, with her good flipper, she swims as rapidly as she can. In circles. The next blow takes her near the

Violently he
swings her . . .

neck, lifting her high out of the water and slapping her down again. She tastes blood in her torn throat as it pours from her severed jugular.

She falls. Plunging into darkness as the leopard seal carries her on a long, deep dive. It is hatching. It is fledging. It is every day of her life. The sea has been her lifeblood, and now she drowns in a suffocating mixture of its water and her own blood.

When the leopard seal reaches the surface, her body is limp, lifeless. He lets her float. Suddenly, viciously, he swings her unresisting body through the air, slapping it into the water in a great arc that sprays a trail of water in its fury. Violently he swings her: two, three, ten, twenty times – as if the leopard seal is intent on bruising the entire body of the sea using my mate as his weapon. Indeed, the water is blotched with blood. Her bones broken, her skin torn, her body literally beaten to a pulp, her nemesis sets about eating her. Tearing large chunks of flesh and feathers, bones and blood, the leopard seal tilts back its head and, facing a god in which it does not believe, it swallows one in which it does. My mate is dead, but through her the leopard seal will live – at least for another day – and what is god, if he is not the giver of life?

It is late summer. A blustery northerly has blown away the many days of cloud. Pack ice eddies along the shore. Behind, huge flat-topped bergs float south, surprisingly quick given their size. They have slutted off the ice shelf. Summer's gift to the sea. Just as the pack ice comes from winter's cold, the icebergs can fracture free of the shelf only after a season of warmth. A subdued sun now loses its intensity, as if giving up its battle to stay above the distant mountains, signaling the end of summer. Soon we penguins will need to move north with the pack ice and bergs, in the wake of a retreating sun. But for the moment, the weaker rays of the sun serve to highlight Antarctica's beauty, her fragile strength.

I have returned briefly to the colony to find and feed my chick. It waits for me on our nest site, too big now to be much bothered by skuas. I will leave again before my feathers dry. Alone I am able to get enough food for my chick and myself, but I must work hard for it. I lean forward and regurgitate. My chick is not quite quick enough and the majority of my vomit spills to the ground. A wasted effort. A meal for the skuas.

My chick spreads its flippers and silently goes through the motions of an *ecstatic* display: its behavior taking shape like its body. Its down is patchy, new feathers showing through underneath. The feathers on its back are a bluish black, while those on its belly and chin are white. Soon my chick will enter the water, not returning to the rookery for two, or even three summers. When it does return, it will come with the black chin of an adult, ready to begin its own uncertain race to make more life in this unforgiving land.

It is not that this land is hostile that makes it so unforgiving. Oh sure, it may be cold and barren; but then again we have feathers, down, and crèches to keep us warm; we have continuous daylight for feeding and a plankton bloom for food. No, it is not its hostility, but its vulnerability that makes Antarctica the unforgiving land. We who live here walk a fine line, with death on one side, and death on the other.

As I stand on a vestige of the push ice, washed yellow by the late season sun, I hesitate momentarily before diving into the sea. It is not grief at the loss of my chick or mate that gives me pause, it is not the dangers of either the leopard seal or another approaching winter that frightens me, it is the thud-thud-thud of helicopter blades.

GLOSSARY

Adélie penguin Named after the wife of French explorer Durmont d'Urville, this penguin lives and breeds only on the coast and islands around Antarctica.

Alternate stare Movement of the head from side to side, presenting alternate eyes to an intruder when approached closely. It is a display that conveys a mixture of anxiety and aggressiveness.

Arms act The waving of flippers and vibrating of the bill by a male as he walks backward along the female's back during copulation.

Bloom Massive levels of abundance of plankton when they undergo rapid population growth in response to seasonally variable conditions.

Breeding season Adélie penguins start arriving at Cape Bird in late October to early November. They must get from courtship to fledging their young within three months. The chicks fledge in late January to mid February.

Brood patch Area of bare skin on the underside of a bird against which eggs are incubated. It is infused with blood vessels thereby providing an avenue for transfer of heat from the parent to the egg. Brood patches develop around the time of egg laying in response to hormonal changes.

Cape Bird The northern tip of Ross Island. Site of three penguin rookeries that are virtually as far south as any penguin breeds (the only sites farther south are also on Ross Island).

Cloaca Terminal part of the gut into which the kidney and reproductive ducts open; unlike mammals there is a single posterior opening to the body, the cloacal aperture, rather than separate anal and urinogenital openings.

Colony A breeding group of penguins in which nests are contiguous. Mean distance between nests is about 28 inches.

Crèche A group of three or more chicks in close proximity to each other. Chicks usually enter crèches at about three weeks of age, when both parents may be away from the nest simultaneously to get food for them. Although the chicks may derive some protection from the cold by standing in contact or near each other, crèches mostly provide protection from predators such as skuas. Prior to the crèche stage, chicks are guarded by one parent remaining on the nest at all times.

Ecstatic display A display given mostly by males, and exclusively by them during the courtship period. It is most prevalent in unattached males and serves a function in attracting females. Displaying males are likely to induce other males to display, and this social facilitation could help synchronize the breeding schedule of the penguins in the short Antarctic summer.

Hormones Chemical messengers produced in one part of the body that effect a response in another part. Hormones are conveyed via the bloodstream.

Incubation The period of development of a bird's embryo that occurs within the egg between laying and hatching. For development to occur the eggs must be kept warm, requiring a parent to keep them against its brood patch–an area of skin infused with blood vessels. Incubation in the Adélie penguin takes about 34 days.

Krill Small shrimplike crustaceans that are the significant component of the zooplankton in Antarctic waters and the key species in the Antarctic ecosystem.

Lead Channel of open water between floes of pack ice.

Molt The process when old feathers are replaced by new feathers. This occurs annually at the end of the breeding season.

Mutual display This display occurs between a pair usually when reuniting at the nest site. The birds vocalize while waving their heads from side to side. Sometimes this Loud Mutual Display, as it is often called, is given by a lone bird to its eggs or chicks. The calls of individuals are distinctive. A less intense version of the mutual display with a much softer call is known as the Quiet Mutual.

Oates "Titus" Oates (1880–1912). British explorer who accompanied Scott on his trek to the South Pole. On the return journey he developed badly frostbitten feet. His condition worsened and, rather than be a burden to his companions, he met his end by walking out into a blizzard. Scott recorded Oates's last words in his diary as, "I am just going outside and may be some time."

Porpoising Fastest swimming mode of penguins. Involves alternately swimming several strokes underwater and then taking a breath as the body is propelled through the air. Penguins use their flippers for propulsion. They are able to swim at up to 10 miles per hour using this method.

Rookery A group of adjacent penguin colonies confined to a particular geographic area. For other species of birds this is equivalent to what would be called a "colony," while the colonies themselves are equivalent to "breeding groups."

Ross Island A volcanic island in the Ross Sea permanently joined to the Antarctic continent by the Ross Ice Shelf. It was the staging post for the expeditions of Scott and Shackleton. Today it is the site of the New Zealand Antarctic Program's Scott Base and the United States Antarctic Program's McMurdo Station.

Scott Robert Falcon Scott (1868–1912). British explorer who led two expeditions to Antarctica with the aim of being the first person to reach the South Pole. On his second expedition he succeeded in reaching the pole on January 17, 1912, only to discover that he had been beaten by a party lead by Norwegian explorer Roald Amundsen who had arrived at the pole one month earlier. On the return journey, Scott and all members of his party ("Birdie" Bowers, Edgar Evans, "Titus" Oates, and Edward Wilson) perished. Scott, Wilson and Bowers died of starvation and exhaustion only 11 miles from a food supply depot.

Skua Large, brown gull-like birds, South Polar Skuas breed on the Antarctic continent and some nearby islands. They feed predominantly on fish. However, they are strongly territorial, and where they nest in association with penguin colonies, those skuas with penguin nests within their breeding territories may take penguin eggs and chicks. During the winter period they undergo long migrations that expose them to pesticides and industrial contaminants.

Winter migration Outside of the breeding season Adélie penguins travel north with the pack ice. Tracking by satellites has shown that the penguins at Cape Bird may go to areas over 1,000 miles from the rookery, though the actual distance they travel during the course of the migration would probably exceed 3,000 miles.